MINDFULNESS WHILE

PLAYING SPORTS

PRISCILLA AN

childsworld.com

The Child's World®
childsworld.com

Published by The Child's World®
800-599-READ · www.childsworld.com

Photography Credits
Photographs ©: Monkey Business Images/Shutterstock
Images, cover, 1, 14–15, 16, 19, 20; Shutterstock Images, 3,
5, 6–7, 8–9, 11, 13; iStockphoto, 22

ISBN Information
9781503869622 (Reinforced Library Binding)
9781503880924 (Portable Document Format)
9781503882232 (Online Multi-user eBook)
9781503883543 (Electronic Publication)
9781645498674 (Paperback)

LCCN 2022951199

Printed in the United States of America

Priscilla An is a children's book
editor and author. She lives in
Minnesota with her rabbit and
likes to practice mindfulness
through yoga.

TABLE OF CONTENTS

WHAT IS MINDFULNESS?

Playing or learning a new sport is fun. But sometimes, negative emotions such as anger and fear can come up. These emotions can **distract** people from enjoying the game or activity. Mindfulness can help. Mindfulness is when people are aware of their thoughts, feelings, and surroundings. Being mindful can help a person **focus** on a game. It can help people calm down.

Practicing mindfulness can keep distractions at bay.

MISSED GOAL

Kyle plays soccer. His team, the Red Dragons, is playing against the Sparks. The Sparks already scored one goal. Kyle's team does not have any goals yet.

A teammate passes Kyle the ball. Kyle's heart races. His palms are sweating. He is nervous about having the ball. He does not want to disappoint his team.

Teamwork is important in soccer.

In soccer, a team scores by kicking the ball into the goal.

Kyle **dribbles** the ball toward the goal. Before he shoots, he pauses to look around. Players from the other team are running toward him, but he has a clear shot.

Kyle kicks the ball. He misses the net. The Sparks cheer. Kyle looks at his teammates. They look upset. The referee blows her whistle. It is the end of the first half of the game.

Kyle is angry at himself. It was such an easy goal. He should have made it! He does not want to face his teammates. Hot tears start to trickle down his face.

Coach Sam walks over to Kyle. He puts his hand on Kyle's shoulder. "Are you OK?" he asks.

Kyle shakes his head. "I can't believe I missed the goal. It was so easy!"

"Can you tell me more about how you feel?" Coach Sam asks.

"I feel embarrassed that I missed that shot. I also feel mad at myself," Kyle sniffles.

Coach Sam nods. "I understand how frustrating it can be to miss a goal. It can be hard to let go of those negative feelings. But focusing on positive feelings can help. What made you come out to play today? Why do you play soccer?"

Coaches can give helpful advice.

IN THE ZONE

Many **professional** athletes practice mindfulness. They know the importance of training their bodies and their minds. When they are focused on the present moment, they are able to play their best. This helps them ignore the "what if" situations. They can focus on their goals.

"I like playing with my team. It's really fun," Kyle says.

Coach Sam pats Kyle's shoulder. "That's great! Soccer is fun, and so is playing with your team. Can you try something with me? First, we can breathe in, accepting the feelings of embarrassment and anger."

Coach Sam closes his eyes and puts his hand on his stomach. He breathes in deeply. Kyle watches Coach's belly expand with the breath. Kyle closes his eyes and breathes in. He allows his negative feelings to come up in his mind.

"Now you can breathe out. Let go of those feelings," Coach Sam says. Kyle breathes out. He sends the thoughts away. He thinks about how much fun he has playing with his team. He focuses on the parts of soccer that make him happy.

Teammates can encourage each other.

Kyle opens his eyes. He feels like something heavy was lifted off his chest. He feels like he can play again. "Thanks, Coach!"

Kyle runs back to his team. His teammates all **huddle** around him. "Good job, Kyle!" they say. "We can try again!"

Kyle feels **encouraged**. He smiles at everyone. "Thanks, guys!" He raises a fist in the air. "Let's go, Red Dragons!" The rest of his teammates cheer loudly.

LETTING GO OF FEAR

It is Terri's first day of swim class. The other kids in the class are excited. But Terri feels nervous. She has never been swimming before. Ian is the swim teacher. He tells the students that it is normal to be scared. But he adds that anyone can learn to swim. He will help them. Ian promises that every single person will be safe.

Swimming for the first time can be scary.

Taking a swim class can be fun.

As Terri listens, she begins to feel scared. She has heard stories of people drowning. What if that happens to her? Her stomach starts to hurt.

It is time for everyone to go into the water. Terri's friend Jesse splashes her.

"This is fun!" Jesse laughs. Terri tries to smile at him. But the water feels cold against her skin. Her body shakes. She is still scared.

Ian passes yellow kickboards to everyone. He tells them to hold the board with their arms straight. They are going to practice kicking across the pool.

Terri holds her board tightly. Even though her body is floating, she is scared that she will fall off. Her breaths are short and **panicky**. Ian swims next to her. "Hey Terri, take a moment to stop and breathe. I am right here. I can help you float."

Terri slowly inhales and exhales. With each breath, she notices the things around her. The blue water looks like the color of the sky. She feels warmer than before. Her body feels lighter. She knows her teacher is right here. He will help if she starts to sink. Terri slowly starts to kick. She feels herself move forward. Terri relaxes her grip on her board. She kicks harder. She likes how the water sounds when she kicks really hard.

Terri makes it to the other side of the pool. She feels much better. She does not feel scared anymore.

Kickboards help people float.

FEAR IS NORMAL

Fear is a normal response that everyone has. People do not need to feel embarrassed when they are afraid. Instead, they can try welcoming their fear and noticing how it feels. Then they can try letting it go.

Swimming is a fun way to exercise.

After the class ends, Terri grabs her towel and wraps it around her shoulders. She feels proud of herself. Ian tells the class what a great job they did. He says next time, they are going to practice putting their faces in the water! Everyone is excited for their next class.

Practicing mindfulness helped Terri focus on her body rather than on her fear. It helped her thoughts rest. She did not think about drowning anymore. She might feel scared again, but she knows she can **overcome** it.

WONDER MORE

Wondering about New Information

How much did you know about the importance of pausing and breathing deeply before reading this book? What new information did you learn? Write down two new facts that this book taught you. Was the new information surprising? Why or why not?

Wondering How It Matters

What is one way being mindful while playing sports relates to your life? How do you think being mindful while playing sports relates to other kids' lives?

Wondering Why

Noticing and letting go of fear is important. Why do you think it is important to do both? How might knowing this affect your life?

Ways to Keep Wondering

Learning about mindfulness while playing sports can be a complex topic. After reading this book, what questions do you have about it? What can you do to learn more about mindfulness?

TOUCH AND LET GO

When fear feels like it might take over, try this activity.

 1 Notice the fear. Do not push it away. How is fear showing up in your body? Is your heart beating quickly? Do your hands feel sweaty?

2 Take three slow, deep breaths.

3 Think about your fear. What is your fear about? Imagine that you are putting your fear into your hands. Close your hands around your fear.

4 Open up your hands and imagine that you are letting your fears go, like letting a balloon float away.

GLOSSARY

distract (dih-STRAKT) To distract is to turn someone's attention away from something. Feeling embarrassed and angry can distract people from playing their best.

dribbles (DRIH-buhls) When someone dribbles a soccer ball, he is lightly kicking it. Kyle dribbles the ball down the field.

encouraged (en-KUR-ijd) To feel encouraged is to feel hopeful and confident. Kyle felt encouraged when his teammates tried to cheer him up.

focus (FOH-kuss) To focus is to pay special attention to something. Negative feelings can make it hard to focus on playing a sport.

huddle (HUH-duhl) To huddle is to gather closely together. Kyle's teammates huddle around him to make him feel better.

overcome (oh-vur-KUHM) When people overcome their fears, it means that they can defeat or get over them. Terri was able to overcome her fear of swimming by practicing mindfulness.

panicky (PAN-ik-ee) When someone feels panicky, she is experiencing panic, or feelings of intense fear. Ian calmed Terri's panicky breathing by helping her breathe slowly.

professional (proh-FEH-shuh-null) To be professional is to be paid to do something. Professional athletes play sports as a job.

response (rih-SPAHNSE) A response is something that happens because of something else. Fear is a normal response to new activities.

FIND OUT MORE

In the Library

An, Priscilla. *Mindfulness on the Playground*.
Parker, CO: The Child's World, 2024.

Minden, Cecilia. *Coaches*. Parker, CO:
The Child's World, 2023.

Sileo, Frank J. *A World of Pausabilities: An Exercise in Mindfulness*. Washington, DC: Magination Press, 2017.

On the Web

Visit our website for links about mindfulness while playing sports:
childsworld.com/links

Note to Parents, Caregivers, Teachers, and Librarians: We routinely verify our Web links to make sure they are safe and active sites. So encourage your readers to check them out!

INDEX